ENDANGERED AND THREATENED ANIMALS

THE
MANATEE

A MyReportLinks.com Book

John Albert Torres

MyReportLinks.com Books
an imprint of
 Enslow Publishers, Inc. E
Box 398, 40 Industrial Road
Berkeley Heights, NJ 07922
USA

T 31964

L

MyReportLinks.com Books, an imprint of Enslow Publishers, Inc. MyReportLinks®
is a trademark of Enslow Publishers, Inc.

Library of Congress Cataloging-in-Publication Data

Torres, John Albert.
  The manatee / John Albert Torres.
    p. cm. — (Endangered and threatened animals)
Summary: Discusses what manatees are, why they are endangered, what
their current status is, and what is being done to help them. Includes
Internet links to Web sites related to manatees.
Includes bibliographical references (p.   ).
  ISBN 0-7660-5173-0
  1. Manatees—Juvenile literature. 2. Endangered species—Juvenile
literature. [1. Manatees. 2. Endangered species.] I. Title. II. Series.

  QL737.S63T67 2004
  599.55—dc22

                            2003016365

Printed in the United States of America

10 9 8 7 6 5 4 3 2 1

To Our Readers:
Through the purchase of this book, you and your library gain access to the Report Links that specifically back
up this book.
The Publisher will provide access to the Report Links that back up this book and will keep these Report Links
up to date on **www.myreportlinks.com** for three years from the book's first publication date.
We have done our best to make sure all Internet addresses in this book were active and appropriate when we
went to press. However, the author and the Publisher have no control over, and assume no liability for, the
material available on those Internet sites or on other Web sites they may link to.
The usage of the MyReportLinks.com Books Web site is subject to the terms and conditions stated on the
Usage Policy Statement on **www.myreportlinks.com**.
In the future, a password may be required to access the Report Links that back up this book. The password
is found on the bottom of page 4 of this book.
Any comments or suggestions can be sent by e-mail to comments@myreportlinks.com or to the address on
the back cover.

Photo Credits: *ClickArt 200,000*, p. 10; © 1998–2002 Michael T. Bragg, pp. 19, 42; © 2001–2002
State of Florida, pp. 30, 34; © 2002 Busch Entertainment Corporation, pp. 12, 15; © Corel
Corporation, pp. 3, 11, 16, 21, 22, 26, 32, 38, 39; © Great Barrier Reef Marine Park Authority 1996,
p. 36; John Bavaro, p. 18; MyReportLinks.com Books, p. 3; Photos.com, pp. 1, 29, 40; Save the
Manatee Club, p. 33; U.S. Fish and Wildlife Service, p. 45; USGS — Sirenia Project, pp. 13, 20, 25.

Cover Photo: © Corel Corporation

Contents

MyReportLinks.com Books
Great Books, Great Links, Great for Research!

The Report Links listed on the following four pages can save you hours of research time by **instantly** bringing you to the best Web sites relating to your report topic.

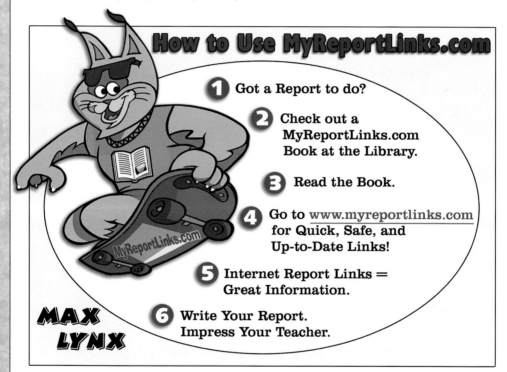

How to Use MyReportLinks.com

1 Got a Report to do?

2 Check out a MyReportLinks.com Book at the Library.

3 Read the Book.

4 Go to www.myreportlinks.com for Quick, Safe, and Up-to-Date Links!

5 Internet Report Links = Great Information.

6 Write Your Report. Impress Your Teacher.

MAX LYNX

The pre-evaluated Web sites are your links to source documents, photographs, illustrations, and maps. They also provide links to dozens—even hundreds—of Web sites about your report subject.

MyReportLinks.com Books and the MyReportLinks.com Web site save you time and make report writing easier than ever!

Please see "To Our Readers" on the copyright page for important information about this book, the MyReportLinks.com Web site, and the Report Links that back up this book. Please enter **EMA3523** if asked for a password.

Report Links

The Internet sites described below can be accessed at
http://www.myreportlinks.com

*EDITOR'S CHOICE

⌐ Manatees
SeaWorld's Web site contains information on the manatee's behavior,
eating habits, communication, and more.

Link to this Internet site from http://www.myreportlinks.com

*EDITOR'S CHOICE

⌐ Fast Facts
This site provides basic facts about the manatee, plus a section
discussing threats to the manatee's existence. There are tips for
what can be done to help these animals.

Link to this Internet site from http://www.myreportlinks.com

*EDITOR'S CHOICE

⌐ Animal Info: American Manatee
On this site, you can read a brief description of what the American
manatee looks like, as well as information on its other characteristics
and habits.

Link to this Internet site from http://www.myreportlinks.com

*EDITOR'S CHOICE

⌐ Manatee
This site takes you on a virtual journey to Homosassa Springs and
Crystal River, Florida, to meet the manatee. Included are dozens of
photos and engaging stories.

Link to this Internet site from http://www.myreportlinks.com

*EDITOR'S CHOICE

⌐ The Official Web Site of Save the Manatee Club
The Save the Manatee Club Web site provides information on
manatees and the efforts to help protect them in the wild.

Link to this Internet site from http://www.myreportlinks.com

*EDITOR'S CHOICE

⌐ Manatee Coast
This site provides detailed information on the Florida manatee. Be sure
to check out the tracking center to get the location of two manatees the
zoo released with GPS transmitters.

Link to this Internet site from http://www.myreportlinks.com

The Internet sites described below can be accessed at
http://www.myreportlinks.com

All About Manatees
This site provides general manatee information. There are also links to a
research project in Belize where people are studying the Antillean manatee.

Link to this Internet site from http://www.myreportlinks.com

Call of the Siren
This page provides information on manatee research and conservation. It also
includes links to other manatee-related sites.

Link to this Internet site from http://www.myreportlinks.com

Facts about Dugongs
This Web site provides general information on the dugong, a close relative to
the manatee.

Link to this Internet site from http://www.myreportlinks.com

The Florida Manatee
This article contains information on the Florida manatee and what is being
done to help protect the species.

Link to this Internet site from http://www.myreportlinks.com

**Florida Fish and Wildlife Conservation Commission:
Manatee Program**
On this site from the Bureau of Protected Species Management, you will find
out what the state of Florida is doing in their manatee conservation efforts.

Link to this Internet site from http://www.myreportlinks.com

Florida (West Indian) Manatee
This site provides general information on the Florida manatee and the reasons
why it has become endangered.

Link to this Internet site from http://www.myreportlinks.com

Report Links

▶ The Internet sites described below can be accessed at
http://www.myreportlinks.com

▶ **Homosassa Springs Wildlife Park**
Homosassa Springs Wildlife Park is a safe haven for injured or
orphaned manatees and for those born in captivity. Their Web site
contains general information on manatees and about the work of
the park.

Link to this Internet site from http://www.myreportlinks.com

▶ *Hydrodamalis gigas:* **Steller's Sea Cow**
Steller's Sea Cow, which was in the same scientific order as the
manatee, became extinct in the late 1700s. This mammal was
found mostly in the Northern Pacific Ocean.

Link to this Internet site from http://www.myreportlinks.com

▶ **The Jane and David Allen Manatee Exhibit**
This site contains information on Hugh and Buffett, two manatees that
were born in captivity and are on display at the Mote Marine
Laboratory in Sarasota, Florida.

Link to this Internet site from http://www.myreportlinks.com

▶ **Kids Only: Manatees & Dugongs**
This site takes a look at the lives of the manatee and dugong.

Link to this Internet site from http://www.myreportlinks.com

▶ **Manatee—Sirenia Project**
The Florida Integrated Science Center conducts research on the
West Indian manatee to learn about its life history, population,
and what it needs to survive. Read about their findings and what is
currently being studied.

Link to this Internet site from http://www.myreportlinks.com

▶ **Manatee:** *Trichechus manatus*
This Web site provides a fact sheet about the manatee containing
information about its size, habitat, diet, life span, and more.

Link to this Internet site from http://www.myreportlinks.com

The Internet sites described below can be accessed at
http://www.myreportlinks.com

Manatee Conservation
The Dolphin Research Center provides information on conservation efforts
and the threats that exist to manatees.

Link to this Internet site from http://www.myreportlinks.com

Manatee Information Sheet
This site contains information on the manatee's description, distribution,
habitat, and more.

Link to this Internet site from http://www.myreportlinks.com

Manatee Overview
This site from the Florida Power and Light Company Web site provides
information and resources on the Florida manatee. It includes guidelines
for boating and jet-skiing in areas where manatees live.

Link to this Internet site from http://www.myreportlinks.com

Manatee Photographs
View several photographs of the West Indian manatee in its natural environment.

Link to this Internet site from http://www.myreportlinks.com

Marine Mammal Protection Act (MMPA) of 1972
On this site you will find the complete text of the Marine Mammal Protection
Act of 1972.

Link to this Internet site from http://www.myreportlinks.com

Monsters or Mermaids?
This site from PBS describes the history of the manatee, beginning with
ancient sailors who mistook these mammals for mermaids. It also discusses
how the government is trying to prevent the manatee from becoming extinct.

Link to this Internet site from http://www.myreportlinks.com

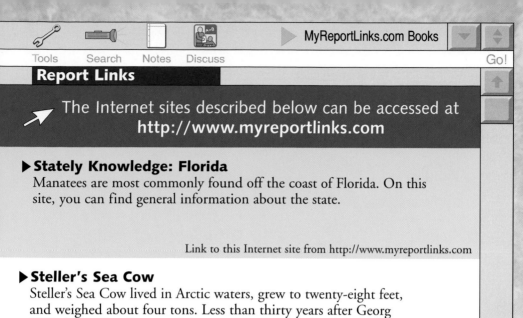
Report Links

The Internet sites described below can be accessed at
http://www.myreportlinks.com

▶ **Stately Knowledge: Florida**
Manatees are most commonly found off the coast of Florida. On this site, you can find general information about the state.

Link to this Internet site from http://www.myreportlinks.com

▶ **Steller's Sea Cow**
Steller's Sea Cow lived in Arctic waters, grew to twenty-eight feet, and weighed about four tons. Less than thirty years after Georg Wilhelm Steller discovered this species in 1741, they became extinct.

Link to this Internet site from http://www.myreportlinks.com

▶ **U.S. Fish and Wildlife Service: The Endangered Species Act of 1973**
Access the entire Endangered Species Act of 1973 on the U.S. Fish and Wildlife Service Web site.

Link to this Internet site from http://www.myreportlinks.com

▶ **Walker's Mammals of the World: Manatees**
This Web site from John Hopkins University provides information on the characteristics of the West Indian, Amazonian, and West African manatees.

Link to this Internet site from http://www.myreportlinks.com

▶ **West Indian Manatee**
This site houses general information on the West Indian manatee. You can also view a map that shows the distribution of manatees throughout the world.

Link to this Internet site from http://www.myreportlinks.com

▶ **The Wonderful World of the Manatee**
This site includes information on the manatee, as well as what you can do to help save the manatee from extinction.

Link to this Internet site from http://www.myreportlinks.com

Class
Mammalia

Family
Trichechid AE.

Genus
Trichechus

Species
Sirenians

Average Length
10 feet (3 meters)

Average Weight
800 to 1,200 pounds (362.9 to 544.3 kilograms)

Life Span
50 to 60 years

Status
Florida (West Indian) manatee is endangered.
Amazonian manatee is endangered.
West African manatee is threatened.

Skin Color
Grayish brown

Breeding Season
Year round

Gestation Period
12 months

Offspring
One every three years.
Occasionally there are twins.

Range
Florida (West Indian) manatee are mostly found in FL, GA, Puerto Rico, Mexico and in the Caribbean Sea.
Amazonian manatee are found at the Amazon River basin in South America.
West African manatee are found along the west coast of Africa.

Maximum Speed
15 miles per hour (24.1 kilometers per hour)

Threats to Survival
Boats, pollution, loss of habitat

Voice
Can make sounds to communicate to their young, and each other in times of danger.

All metric measurements are estimates.

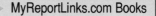
Sea Cows

Visitors to the famous SeaWorld theme park in Orlando, Florida, are thrilled time after time by killer whale extravaganzas and dolphin acrobatics. At the same time, they are humbled by the manatee exhibit called "Manatees: The Last Generation?"

A cornerstone of the park, the manatee exhibit introduces visitors to the gentle sea cow with a film set in the near future where manatees no longer exist. Luckily, that has not taken place. Visitors are then shown huge tanks where the gigantic seal-like mammals interact with each

▲ Manatees are gentle creatures that some people call sea cows.

other, often eating lettuce and staring at their new human friends. SeaWorld is one of the few places allowed by the United States government to rescue and rehabilitate injured or sick manatees. Sometimes the SeaWorld marine biologists even take the sick or injured animals back to the theme park until they are better. Visitors leave the park with a sense that the extinction of manatees, though a possibility, can be avoided.

▶ Mermaids?

Things were not always like this for the *Trichechus manatus latirostris*, or Florida manatee. The Florida manatee is a subspecies of the West Indian manatee. Their numbers were

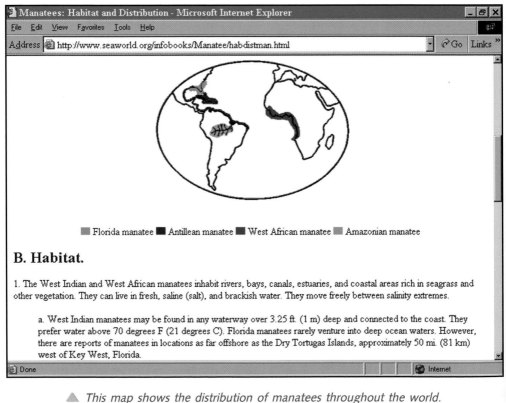

Manatees: Habitat and Distribution - Microsoft Internet Explorer

File Edit View Favorites Tools Help

Address http://www.seaworld.org/infobooks/Manatee/habdistman.html Go Links

■ Florida manatee ■ Antillean manatee ■ West African manatee ■ Amazonian manatee

B. Habitat.

1. The West Indian and West African manatees inhabit rivers, bays, canals, estuaries, and coastal areas rich in seagrass and other vegetation. They can live in fresh, saline (salt), and brackish water. They move freely between salinity extremes.

a. West Indian manatees may be found in any waterway over 3.25 ft. (1 m) deep and connected to the coast. They prefer water above 70 degrees F (21 degrees C). Florida manatees rarely venture into deep ocean waters. However, there are reports of manatees in locations as far offshore as the Dry Tortugas Islands, approximately 50 mi. (81 km) west of Key West, Florida.

Done Internet

▲ *This map shows the distribution of manatees throughout the world. Included are the ranges for all four species of the manatee.*

Tools   Search   Notes   Discuss   Go!

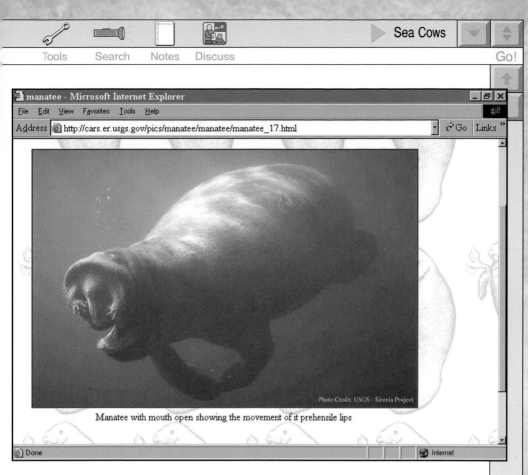

manatee - Microsoft Internet Explorer

File   Edit   View   Favorites   Tools   Help

Address   http://cars.er.usgs.gov/pics/manatee/manatee/manatee_17.html   Go   Links

Photo Credit: USGS - Sirenia Project

Manatee with mouth open showing the movement of it prehensile lips

Done   Internet

Manatees use their uniquely-shaped lips to pull sea grass from the sea floor.

once so big that pirates and sailors at first mistook the one-thousand-pound mammals for mermaids, the mythical half-human half-fish sea creatures. Some people call manatees sea cows. The large mammals swim gracefully and effortlessly much like the mermaids depicted in cartoons and movies. In fact, even explorer Christopher Columbus claimed to have seen mermaids in the Caribbean Sea on his way to the West Indies. He told friends however, that these "mermaids" were not as beautiful as he had seen in paintings.[1] What Columbus possibly saw were colonies of manatees!

No, manatees may not be as beautiful as mermaids, but the gentle, fun-loving mammals are beautiful in their own right. Three types of manatees and one species of dugong make up the order of Sirenia. This name came from combining the words sirens and mermaids.

The Florida manatee and the Antillean manatee are subspecies of the West Indian manatee. There are two other species of manatee. They are the West African manatee, and the Amazonian manatee. All three of the species resemble one another. Like the West Indian manatee, the Amazonian manatee is endangered. The West African manatee is in slightly better shape. The U.S. Fish and Wildlife Service lists that species as threatened.

▶ Diet

Manatees and other sirenians are not only unique because of how they look. They are also different because sirenians are the only sea mammals that eat only vegetables. Other sea mammals, such as dolphins, whales, and seals, feed on fish. Manatees, by constantly feeding on sea grasses, help to keep the coastal waterways in Florida clear of heavy vegetation.

Manatees can be found in shallow waters. They can also be found in saltwater and freshwater rivers, bays, canals, and along coastlines. Manatees prefer to remain in water that is between three and seven feet deep and hardly ever go out into water that is twenty feet deep or more.

Manatees typically reach ten feet in length but have been known to grow as long as fourteen feet. At maturity they weigh about one thousand pounds. An adult manatee can eat about 110 pounds (49.9 kilograms) of food in a single day or about 9 percent of its body weight in wet vegetation. That is a lot of sea grass that needs to be eaten to keep a family of manatees alive. That is why the creatures favor warmer coastal waters, like Florida, where thick water vegetation grows year-round.

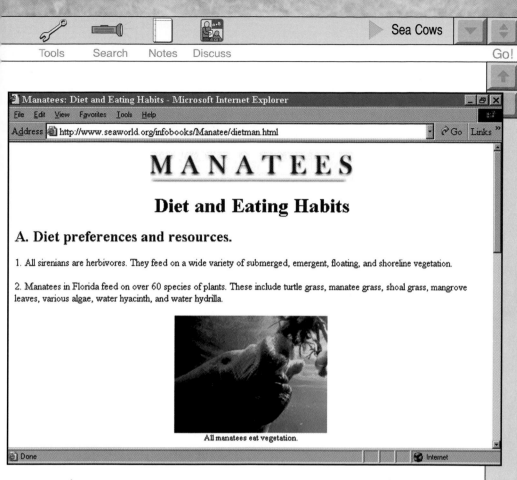

Manatees: Diet and Eating Habits - Microsoft Internet Explorer

File   Edit   View   Favorites   Tools   Help

Address 🔗 http://www.seaworld.org/infobooks/Manatee/dietman.html   🔗 Go   Links »

MANATEES

Diet and Eating Habits

A. Diet preferences and resources.

1. All sirenians are herbivores. They feed on a wide variety of submerged, emergent, floating, and shoreline vegetation.

2. Manatees in Florida feed on over 60 species of plants. These include turtle grass, manatee grass, shoal grass, mangrove leaves, various algae, water hyacinth, and water hydrilla.

All manatees eat vegetation.

Done   🌐 Internet

▲ Manatees are vegetarians, consuming 32 to 108 pounds (4 to 9 percent) of their body weight in wet plants each day.

The manatees make good use of their strong lips. They can move each lip separately. This helps them to grasp and then tear the underwater plants. Sometimes manatees will dig down with their flippers in order to dig out an entire plant and eat the whole thing. A lot of the nutrients, or healthy matter, in the sea grass is in the portion of the plants that is underground.

While plentiful, sea grass is the preferred food of the manatee, but they are certainly not too picky. In fact, manatees have been known to eat up to sixty different types of plants, including mangrove leaves, water hyacinth, and even algae. Basically, they will eat any plant soft enough for their lips to tear from the ground. Scientists have even watched manatees crawl partway out of the water. They do this in order to reach plants that hang down from trees. Sometimes they eat acorns, which are also loaded with nutrients.

▶ Falling Numbers

The gentle sea cow is in trouble. This is despite ideal conditions in certain parts of the world, including Florida, for the manatee to thrive in. Throughout the centuries, manatees were hunted for their fatty meat, oil, and bones. They have been killed by poachers and are often the victims of pollution or cold winters. In the cases of the Amazonian and West African manatee, the biggest cause for the animal's population decline has been loss of habitat. These areas of the world have become more developed. As a result, the number of places where manatees can live has shrunk.

▲ Manatees are slow moving creatures that need to come up for air every once so often. When they do, they are in the most danger of being hit by a boat.

For the Florida manatee, the biggest reason the animal is endangered is because of collisions with boats. Manatees move slowly and need to come up for air. This means it is very difficult for them to move out of the way of oncoming boats. They live in shallow coastal areas. Millions of people use their boats all along Florida's shores, in the same areas where the Florida manatee thrives. According to the Manatee Salvage Program, more than 1,200 of 4,000 manatees they found dead had died directly because of boat accidents. It is rare to find a manatee that does not carry a propeller scar on its back.

No one knows for sure how many manatees are left in Florida, but most experts say the number is less than four thousand. A harsh winter or continued conflicts with boaters could see that number drop in a hurry.[2]

Efforts to protect the Florida manatee have been ongoing. The movement to save the manatee, though, has grown since the Florida Manatee Sanctuary Act was passed in 1978. Soon after, the popular Save the Manatee Club was established in 1981. However, battles with boat enthusiasts and challenges to conservation efforts in Florida's courts continue to put the gentle marine mammal in peril. Now, it seems as if the manatee's future lies in the hands of humankind.

Special Characteristics

Driving along Patrick Drive in Brevard County, Florida, one can see several cars pulled over to the side of the road. The cars are stopped just a short distance from the Atlantic Ocean and the intercoastal waterway. About ten people have gotten out of their cars and are pointing down to a shallow canal. The canal exists to protect the area's homes from flooding during the rainy season. There, in the warm waters, nearly twenty manatees have gathered to munch on some vegetation. Then something curious happens. They begin to play something that resembles "follow the leader." The visitors laugh in amazement before getting back into their cars and heading away.[1]

▶ Friendly Creatures

Manatees seem just fine traveling in small groups doing nothing but eating and resting. Other times they gather in

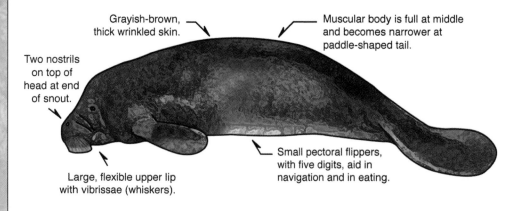

Grayish-brown, thick wrinkled skin.

Muscular body is full at middle and becomes narrower at paddle-shaped tail.

Two nostrils on top of head at end of snout.

Small pectoral flippers, with five digits, aid in navigation and in eating.

Large, flexible upper lip with vibrissae (whiskers).

▲ This drawing shows the main features of the Florida manatee.

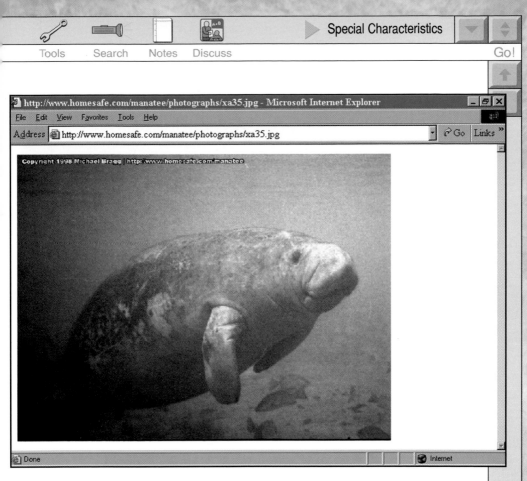

http://www.homesafe.com/manatee/photographs/xa35.jpg - Microsoft Internet Explorer

File   Edit   View   Favorites   Tools   Help

Address http://www.homesafe.com/manatee/photographs/xa35.jpg   Go   Links

Copyright 1998 Michael Bragg | http://www.homesafe.com/manatee

Done   Internet

▲ *When they are underwater, manatee's hearts slow down so they do not have to pump as much blood. This saves them oxygen.*

big groups and play. During "follow the leader," two or more manatees swim together in single file turning, diving, breathing, and changing direction at the exact same time. When the game is over, the animals slow down and nuzzle each other, as if to say "that was fun!"

▶ Underwater

Manatees may look slightly like seals or walruses. Yet, they are a unique animal that has many special characteristics that set them apart. Like most marine mammals, manatees are equipped with special features that allow them to conserve oxygen while underwater. These features allow the animals to stay underwater for longer periods of time. Having a heart that slows down while diving is one of those features. This means that the heart does not have to work as hard pumping blood through the manatee's big body. This saves them precious oxygen.

Unlike whales and dolphins, though, manatees are not equipped to dive down deep. Manatee muscles lack high concentrations of an oxygen-binding protein called myoglobin, which dolphins and whales have. Myoglobin helps these animals stay underwater for long periods of time. Perhaps

manatee - Microsoft Internet Explorer

File Edit View Favorites Tools Help

Address http://cars.er.usgs.gov/pics/manatee/manatee/manatee_3.html   Go Links »

Photo Credit: USGS - Sirenia Project

Underwater view of manatee surfacing to take a breath

Internet

▲ When manatees breathe, they renew about 90 percent of the air in their lungs. This is one reason why they are able to stay underwater for about three minutes at a time.

▲ *Because they have very small eyes, manatees do not have very good vision. This photo shows that they almost always look as if they are squinting.*

as a result, manatees rarely are seen in water more than twenty feet deep.

Manatees normally stay underwater for two to three minutes at a time. Although, their big lungs enable them to stay below the surface for more than twenty minutes if needed. One of the reasons they can do this is because when manatees breathe, they renew about 90 percent of the air in their lungs. When humans breathe, we only renew about 10 percent of our air.

Manatees spend their entire lives in the water, unlike seals and walruses who come out and spend time on land as well. Because of this, manatees are very agile and can

▲ Some experts believe that the manatee is more closely related to the elephant than to any other animal.

maneuver surprisingly well for an animal with its size and girth. Although they travel slowly, averaging about two to six miles per hour, (3.2 to 9.7 kilometers per hour) they have been seen swimming at speeds up to fifteen miles per hour (24.1 kilometers per hour) for short bursts. With no natural predators in Florida, the manatees can take their time going about their business.

▶ Vision

Manatees also have small eyes. When looking at the large sea creature, it seems as if the eyes are too small for their big bodies. However, the little eyes give the manatees excellent close vision for short distances. This is especially important since they spend most of their time in cloudy and muddy waters. However, because their eyes are so small, they do not have good vision for distances. This means they cannot see an oncoming boat until it is very close to the animal, which puts the manatee in danger. Their eyes contain both rod cells and cone cells. This means the animal can see the same in dim light and bright light, daytime and nighttime. There is also a membrane, a piece of very thin skin, that comes down over the eye to protect it.

▶ Hearing

What the manatee lacks in distance vision however, it makes up for with incredible hearing. This is remarkable because when you look at a manatee, there seems to be something missing: ears! In fact, manatees are able to hear from tiny holes just behind their eyes. Dolphins and whales have similar hearing organs. These little holes seem to work best underwater where sound travels six times better than it does in air.

Hearing is especially important for manatee mothers and their calves. The two often make sounds to each other so they always know where the other is. This is important in keeping them together. There are some scientists who feel that manatees do not hear from the holes behind their eyes but rather from an area near their large cheekbones. The manatee's cheekbones are large and oily and come in direct contact with the animal's ear bones. More research is being done to determine exactly how the animal is able to hear.

Manatees fine hearing, though, is not too helpful to them when it comes to avoiding boats. The loud noises from a boat's engine scares manatees. The manatees react by heading to the surface of the water. That is where they are in the most danger of getting hit by a boat's propeller.

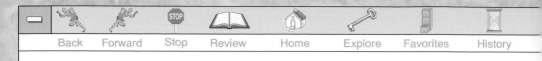
Taste

Their sense of taste can also help them. Scientists agree that manatees probably have a good sense of taste and actually have taste buds in the back of their tongues. Some captive manatees were recently studied at Blue Springs, Florida, to see if they prefer one type of food over another. The manatees did avoid certain plants, such as spatterdock and waterpennywort, that contained toxins or poisons. While Florida manatees eat only vegetation and sometimes nuts, manatees in the Caribbean Sea have been known to go for an easy meal of eating fish caught in nets.

Origins

Strangely enough, the animal that many experts say is the closest relative to the manatee is actually the elephant. Some scientists believe that manatees were once land-dwelling animals and that about 50 million years ago they left the land for the sea. They continued to breathe air but slowly developed their bodies for a life in water.

The reason scientists say that manatees are related to elephants is because they share many of the same special characteristics. Apparently, elephants and manatees have the same types of toenails, teeth, digestive systems, mouth parts, skin, location of mammary glands, and hair. Unfortunately, the manatee also shares another thing in common with one group of elephants, the Asian elephant. They are both listed as endangered species under the Endangered Species Act.

Threats to the Manatee

Humans have a special responsibility when dealing with the delicate balance of nature. It is ultimately up to humans to decide how much of a forest to cut down for wood, when to drain a lake in order to build more houses, or when to put a ban on catching certain types of fish.

manatee - Microsoft Internet Explorer

File   Edit   View   Favorites   Tools   Help

Address 🗿 http://cars.er.usgs.gov/pics/manatee/manatee/manatee_54.html   ⭐ Go   Links »

Two manatees digging in substrate

Done   🌐 Internet

▲ Manatees live in shallow water, such as that of a canal. Being in shallow water gives them enough time to go to the bottom to dig for food for a few minutes, before coming up to breathe.

▲ *There needs to be plenty of coastal grasses in a manatee's habitat. Water pollution can contaminate or destroy these grasses that animals such as this manatee eat to survive.*

▶ Habitat Loss

All these things, and many more, play a huge role in determining how a certain species of animal or plant will survive. In Florida, new home construction is often stopped immediately if there is evidence that scrub-jays—a type of tiny endangered bird—nest in the area.

Sometimes, though, people's needs do not always work out in the animal's best interest. For instance, the number of Amazonian and West African manatees has dropped over the years as humans develop land where the animals live. When a canal is drained in order to build on or develop the land, people sometimes do not think that perhaps the canal was a breeding ground for manatees. Then, the manatees have to find somewhere else to live.

▶ Hunting

In other parts of the world, manatees were hunted for many years for food. Their fatty meat, oil, and bones could be used by a South American or African tribe for a long time. Since the animals are normally curious and do not have a natural fear of man, they are extremely easy to hunt, capture, and kill. Hunting can deplete manatee populations very quickly since their reproduction rate is slow.

A female manatee, or cow, will stay pregnant for twelve months and have one calf every three years. This means they can be effectively wiped out by hunters without ever being able to reproduce.

▶ Pollution

Sometimes destruction of the manatee's habitat can happen even without building new homes or draining wetlands. Sometimes the reason is simply pollution. As Florida's waters become more polluted, two very serious issues are raised for the manatee population. First, pollution along the coastlines can, and has, resulted in contamination or destruction of coastal grasses. The manatees need these grasses to feed upon. This decrease in food supply has led to a smaller manatee population.

Manatees eat between 4 and 9 percent of their body weight every day in vegetation. That means that there needs to be plenty of coastal grasses and available food to keep a group of manatees alive. When food supplies become limited, manatees have to compete with each other for available food. This is not always that important during the summer months. In the winter months, though, manatees need to find warm waters to gather in.

During the winter months, the waters in the Gulf of Mexico and the intercoastal waterway turn colder. Manatees do not like it when water temperatures drop below 68°F. This forces the manatees to seek warmer waters. If they stay in the cold water they can risk catching a respiratory illness, or a cold. This can be fatal for a manatee.

In some parts of Florida, manatees have started to gather outside of power and electrical plants where water discharge is warmer. These artificially heated water sources may help save the manatees. When the animals find such a spot, they do not have to travel to their normal wintering grounds. They are more spread out, so they are less likely to compete for food.

The second issue is that water pollution in recent years has resulted in more red tides. Red tide is caused by an increase in types of algae that release toxins. This occurs naturally every few years. Many times this has no effect on manatees at all. Scientists, however, believe that in recent years, pollution has caused the red tides to become more toxic.[1] The toxicity of the red tides results in manatees dying

▲ *When manatees are more spread out, there is less competition for food. Warm waters outside of electricity plants have become a wintering ground for them.*

as well. Experts say that 20 percent of Florida's manatee population was lost in 1996 when an extremely strong red tide swept through the waters.

▶ Predators

Some scientists believe that sharks may also feed on manatees. However, there is little research on the topic. There is a much bigger threat to the survival of manatees. In addition to water pollution, red tides, and sharks, the biggest threat to the survival of the manatees lies directly with Florida's boating community.

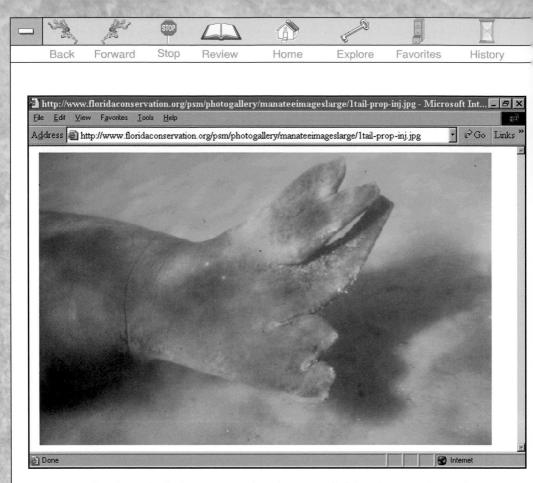

http://www.floridaconservation.org/psm/photogallery/manateeimageslarge/1tail-prop-inj.jpg - Microsoft Int...

Address http://www.floridaconservation.org/psm/photogallery/manateeimageslarge/1tail-prop-inj.jpg

The tail of this manatee has been mauled by the propellers of someone's boat. In order to prevent such accidents, laws have been passed in Florida to enforce reduced speed limits in areas where manatees live.

Boats

Many people move to Florida or vacation there because of the year-round warm weather. This is perfect for those who enjoy boating. The only problem is that boats and manatees often share the same waterways and canals. Many times boats and manatees will collide, and this is a battle the boat will win every time.

In fact, 90 percent of manatee deaths are attributed to collisions with boats. Many of Florida's remaining manatees have visible scars caused by painful collisions with boat propellers. These scars usually heal, and many times the animals are fine. However, if the propeller cuts too close to a vital organ, such as the lungs or the heart, then the animal will die.

Scientists have even started to recognize certain manatees by the scar markings they have on their backs. Since manatees spend up to twelve hours of their day sleeping, many become startled when a speeding boat is approaching. Sleeping manatees are often found near the surface and are in great danger from boats. Remember, manatees have trouble seeing great distances, so they become confused when a loud boat is chugging along. Many times this prevents the animal from getting out of the way. What makes things even more dangerous for manatees is that many of them like to hang around marinas where they suck vegetation off of piers. Sometimes, they like to scratch their backs by rubbing themselves on the bottom of boats. Unsuspecting boaters then start their engines and the propellers hurt the gentle mammals.

Throughout Florida's waterways there are signs reminding boaters that manatees may be present. Manatee safety and boating has become a very political issue in Florida. The state and local governments have taken over in an effort to keep the boating community happy while maintaining a strong manatee population.

Protecting the Manatee

The state of Florida is actively working to pass legislation to help protect the manatee. The large boating community in Florida has sometimes posed a big challenge to lawmakers working to keep the water mammal safe. The main cause of death or injury to manatees remains collisions with boats. As a result, the government has put in place various warnings and regulations regarding the speed of boats.

▶ Boating Regulations

Statistics vary, but the number of manatee deaths each year caused by boat collisions ranges from 35 to 50 percent of

▲ Boating is a popular hobby in coastal states such as Florida. The state has a tough task in trying to protect the manatee, as well as allowing people enjoy the water. These boats are docked in Ft. Lauderdale, Florida.

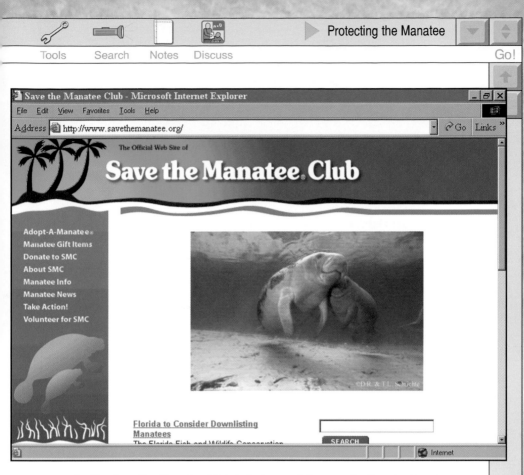

The Save the Manatee Club is just one of the organizations looking to
aid the recovery of manatees in the Southeast United States.

all manatee deaths. Some of the regulations involve what is
called idle speed for boats. This is a very slow speed at
which boats must travel through a manatee protection
zone. There are also slow speed zones where boats are
allowed to travel a little bit faster but are still prohibited
from creating a wake. A wake is a small wave created when
a boat goes by at a fast speed. Wakes make it almost impos-
sible to see the manatees swimming just below the surface.

Boaters are encouraged to wear polarized sunglasses.
These glasses eliminate the glare from the sun and allow
the boater to see just below the water's surface. Boaters are
also encouraged to keep their boats traveling in deep water
channels. They must avoid boating over sea grass beds and

other shallow areas where manatees may be feeding. Boaters are also asked to be alert and watchful. They are asked to keep a sharp lookout for snout, back, or tail that may signal the presence of a manatee. Also, they are encouraged to report injured or sick manatees.

Manatee Refuge

Boaters will even occasionally see a sign that reads: No Entry: Manatee Refuge. This is a protected zone that keeps boaters, swimmers, or divers from entering an area where manatees are known to be.

"More than one million watercraft operators use Florida's waterways annually and the popularity of watercraft

http://www.floridaconservation.org/psm/photogallery/manateeimageslarge/calffeeding.gif - Microsoft Inter...

File   Edit   View   Favorites   Tools   Help

Address   http://www.floridaconservation.org/psm/photogallery/manateeimageslarge/calffeeding.gif   Go   Links

Done   Internet

▲ This mother manatee (right) is feeding her calf. A female manatee is only able to have one calf about every three years.

recreation is continuing to grow," said Jay Slack, field supervisor of the Ecological Services Office for the U.S. Fish and Wildlife Service in Vero Beach, Florida. "Trying to protect manatees from watercraft collisions is one of the most important things we can do to help recover the manatee."[1]

▷ Federal Protection

This sort of protection from unsuspecting boaters could very well be the manatees' last hope. After all, the gentle sea cows were already placed under federal protection back in 1972. Manatees are protected federally under both the Endangered Species Act of 1973 and the Marine Mammal Protection Act of 1972.

These laws prohibit people from harassing, harming, pursuing, hunting, shooting, wounding, trapping, capturing, or killing the animal. The U.S. Fish and Wildlife Service (USFWS) is responsible for posting the signs so that boaters are aware of the danger to manatees. The USFWS also wants to see the speed restrictions enforced. However, it takes money to hire more people, buy more boats, and provide other resources that law-enforcement officials need. Wildlife advocates, however, say the cost is justified. They believe that increase in law enforcement would provide added benefits to the manatees by ensuring that those watercraft already on the water would obey the speed zones currently in place.

"Increased manatee speed zone enforcement is the most important conservation effort we can take to get to a point where life-threatening collisions between manatees and boats are unlikely to occur," Slack said, adding that boater watchfulness is only one of the numerous factors that needs to fall into place to help the mammal recover from danger.

Dugongs are closely related to manatees. They mostly live near the coast of Australia, and are also listed as endangered.

"No one activity alone can recover the manatee. We must work together as a community to recover the manatee."[2]

▶ Reproduction Rate

One of the main reasons why there is pressure on boaters to be careful is that manatees reproduce at a very slow rate. Female manatees are not ready to become mothers until they are around five years old. Males are not ready to become fathers until they are about nine years old. The female manatees usually have only one calf every three years. Twins are very rare.

Because the reproductive rate is so low, manatees as a whole adapt very slowly to changing situations or unnatural stress. One outcome of this is that when boats are going by too quickly or people are harassing the animals, it is very difficult for them to feel comfortable enough to mate.

Do Not Feed the Manatee

Restrictions are not limited to boaters. People wishing the manatees well, and curious tourists, sometimes pose a risk to the animal's well-being. Some people like to feed manatees things like lettuce, or give them a drink of water from a hose. In doing so, they do not realize that they might be encouraging the manatee to swim by and near people who may be cruel to them or wish to hurt them. Also, sometimes manatees may get used to being fed lettuce and water and may start hanging around waiting for more. This can disrupt the manatees' normal feeding patterns and behavior. The animals then become dependent on humans for survival. They may forget how to find their own food or freshwater on their own.

According to conservation officials, feeding manatees is actually considered a form of harassment and so it is against the law. Signs are normally posted where manatees are known to gather. These signs remind visitors that the best way to enjoy manatees is to look but not touch. The signs explain that observing manatees from a distance is a rare opportunity to see the natural behavior of this unique animal.

Take Care of Your Trash

Another way that the Florida Fish and Wildlife Conservation Commission works to protect the manatee is to post reminders to swimmers and boaters that trash left in the waterways is often lethal to manatees, fish, and birds.

▲ *This couple is enjoying fishing off of Captiva Island, Florida. To protect manatee, it is illegal in Florida to put old fishing line in the water. Otherwise, a manatee might strangle itself on the line.*

Plastic bags or six-pack holders are extremely dangerous to the animals. They can suffocate or accidentally strangle themselves. The commission has also started an aggressive campaign to recycle fishing line. There are huge tubes next to most piers and jetties where discarded fishing line and hooks can be placed. Putting old fishing line into the water is against the law in Florida. Manatee and other sea animals may get strangled by the fishing line as well.

The Future

Although the Florida manatee is still listed as endangered, there seems to be good news on the horizon. The animals, because of their protection, have started to recover slightly and are enjoying their best population numbers in a long time. In fact, the numbers have gotten so much better that in December 2002, the Florida Fish and Wildlife Conservation Commission began an extensive biological status review of the manatee.

▲ *This manatee came out of the water to get some sun and air. In Florida, officials attempt to predict how many manatee will live there in the coming years.*

▲ Although efforts to save manatees sometimes cause problems for boaters, the manatee is a beloved creature in Florida.

This means they spent a long time studying everything they could about Florida's manatee population. The commission wanted to see how well the animals were doing and what their prognosis for survival was. One of the reasons this was done was because the criteria for being listed as endangered are not the same on the federal and state levels. The data collected would enable scientists to accurately predict what manatee population levels would be over the next forty-five to one hundred years. This would give the scientists a better idea of whether the manatee faces extinction.

Among the data collected were survival rates, ages of maturity, amounts of red tide, the effects of cold weather, and other factors. This report is the most detailed look at the manatee population to date. What the state found is that it is likely that the manatee population would see a 50 percent decline at some point. To remain on the endangered list, there would need to be an 80 percent decline over the next forty-five years. Extinction within one hundred years did not seem a possibility. So, the news was certainly mixed—not too good, but not too bad either.

▷ Talk of Downlisting

While this is seen as good news for the manatee, the problem is that the Florida Fish and Wildlife Conservation Commission may down-list the animal from endangered to threatened. A survey of manatees in January 2003 showed that there were probably just over three thousand manatees swimming in Florida waters. This was the highest number in years. The Fish and Wildlife people, though, did not want the public to think that the manatees were at healthy population levels. They said that it was very important to note that the "preliminary recommendation for down-listing of the manatee should not be interpreted as confirmation that the species has been 'recovered' or that it no longer requires protection."[1]

The bottom line is that there is a very good chance that the manatee will no longer be considered an endangered animal in Florida. However, this recommendation has nothing to do with the federal listing of the animal as being endangered.

Despite pressure from the boating community, the state decided to delay making a formal announcement of changing the manatee's status. This gives both the boating community and the conservationists plenty of time to continue making their arguments. Boaters want to be able to drive their boats faster and not have to avoid certain

Copyright 1998 Michael Bragg | http://www.homesafe.com/manatee

▲ Conservationists are working hard so that manatees such as this one will be around for generations.

areas of water because they are inhabited by manatees. It is an often bitter battle that has even made its way into Florida's courtrooms.

In March 2003, some angry boaters caused thousands of dollars in damage when they used a chainsaw to cut down signs in the Indian River warning boaters that manatees were present. Police have yet to catch the vandals. It is amazing that such a gentle, seemingly care-free animal can cause such passion on both sides.

▶ Conservation Efforts

The state has even issued special manatee commemorative license plates that are very popular. Every time a Florida resident buys one, the proceeds go to manatee conservation efforts. Other species benefit from these efforts as well. For example, there is also a license plate for those interested in helping to protect the Florida panther, another endangered animal.

One thing, however, is certain: Manatees are doing better than they have in recent years. "We're thrilled by this year's record count of manatees," said Dr. Bruce Ackerman, manatee biologist with the state of Florida. "Based on my past experience, counts can be highly variable due to weather conditions and this year's count isn't entirely unexpected. It seems that everything including perfect weather, survey conditions and the continued support of experience observers combined to make this the best count to date."

Boaters use the high count to try and convince politicians to ease the restrictions placed upon them. Perhaps the best thing that can happen to the manatee is to continuously make the evening news or the daily newspapers. People are reading about manatees, hearing about them,

and talking about them. This causes people to care about the gentle creatures, and most are working to protect them.

Environmental groups are continuously monitoring Florida's waterways to report polluters or reckless boaters. Some even ensure that Florida's numerous floodgates or canal locks are not trapping and drowning manatees in their structures. Because Florida is prone to flooding, there are numerous waterways and canals that manatees wander up into. These canals and waterways protect the public from flooding but sometimes can accidentally cause a manatee to drown.

Despite the risks involved with being taken off the endangered list, Florida's growing and vocal conservationist groups will continue to work hard to ensure that manatees remain in Florida's waters for decades to come. That way, folks can just pull over on South Patrick Drive in Brevard County and watch a dozen or so wild manatees playing in the murky water. If not there, then perhaps all throughout Florida.

The Endangered and Threatened Wildlife List

This series is based on the Endangered and Threatened Wildlife list compiled by the U.S. Fish and Wildlife Service (USFWS). Each book explores an endangered or threatened animal, tells why it has become endangered or threatened, and explains the efforts being made to restore the species' population.

The United States Fish and Wildlife Service, in the Department of the Interior, and the National Marine Fisheries Service, in the Department of Commerce, share responsibility for administration of the Endangered Species Act.

In 1973, Congress took the farsighted step of creating the Endangered Species Act, widely regarded as the world's strongest and most effective wildlife conservation law. It set an ambitious goal: to reverse the alarming trend of human-caused extinction that threatened the ecosystems we all share.

The complete list of Endangered and Threatened Wildlife and Plants can be found at

http://endangered.fws.gov/wildlife.html#Species

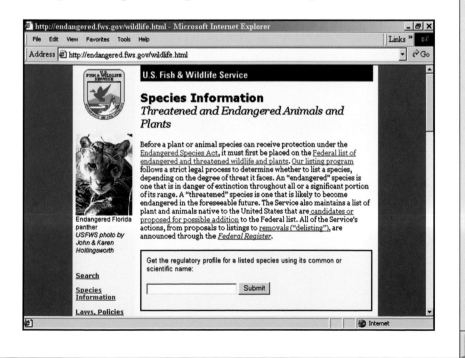

Chapter 1. Sea Cows

1. Time Life Student Library, *Mammals* (Alexandria, Va.: Time Life Books, 1997), p. 119.

2. Information is courtesy of the Dolphin Research Center.

Chapter 2. Special Characteristics

1. An observation by the author, who has visited the area.

Chapter 3. Threats to the Manatee

1. Information courtesy of author conversation with the Florida Marine Research Institute.

Chapter 4. Protecting the Manatee

1. Author interview with Jay Slack, Field Supervisor of the Ecological Services Office for the U.S. Fish & Wildlife Service in Vero Beach, Florida.

2. Ibid.

Chapter 5. The Future

1. Author interview with Jay Slack, Field Supervisor of the Ecological Services Office for the U.S. Fish & Wildlife Service in Vero Beach, Florida.

Further Reading

Bauman, Amy, and Patricia Corrigan. *The Wonder of Manatees.* Milwaukee, Wis.: Gareth Stevens, 2000.

Browntrout Publishers Staff. *Manatees.* San Mateo, Calif.: Browntrout Publishers, 2001.

Dietz, Tim. *The Call of the Siren: Manatees and Dugongs.* Golden, Colo.: Fulcrum, 1992.

Harman, Amanda. *Manatees & Dugongs.* New York: Benchmark Books, 1997.

Jenkins, Priscilla Belz. *A Safe Home for Manatees.* New York: HarperCollins Publishers, 1997.

O'Keefe, M. Timothy. *Manatees: Our Vanishing Mermaids.* Lakeland, Fla.: Larsen's Outdoor Publishing, 1993.

Palazzo-Craig, Janet. *I Can Read About Manatees.* Mahwah, N.J.: Troll Communications, 1999.

Perry, Phyllis J. *Freshwater Giants: Hippopotamuses, River Dolphins, and Manatees.* Danbury, Conn.: Franklin Watts, 2000.

Powell, James. *Manatees: Natural History & Conservation.* Stillwater, Minn.: Voyageur Press, 2003.

Price-Goff, Claire. *The Manatee.* Farmington Hills, Mich.: Gale Group, 1999.

Ripple, Jeff, and Doug Perrine. *Manatees and Dugongs of the World.* Stillwater, Minn.: Voyageur Press, 1999.

Rustad, Martha E. *Manatees.* Mankato, Minn.: Pebble Books, 2003.

Silverstein, Alvin, et al. *The Manatee.* Brookfield, Conn.: Millbrook Press, 1996.

Sleeper, Barbara. *In the Company of Manatees: A Tribute.* New York: Three Rivers Press, 2000.

Walker, Sally M. *Manatees.* Minneapolis, Minn.: Carolrhoda Books, 1999.